CHILDREN'S
BIBLE
CLASSICS

JOSEPH AND THE COAT OF MANY COLORS

Publishers Since 1798

THOMAS NELSON PUBLISHERS
Nashville

First published in 1994 by
Thomas Nelson Publishers, Nashville, Tennessee.

**Story retold by Bill Yenne
and Timothy Jacobs**

Art and design direction by Bill Yenne. Illustrated by Mark Busacca, Edwin Esquivel, Emi Fukawa, Doug Scott, Vadim Vahrameev, Hanako Wakiyama, and Bill Yenne. Special thanks to Ruth DeJauregui.

Produced by
Bluewood Books (A Division of The Siyeh Group, Inc.)
P.O. Box 460313, San Francisco, CA 94146

Yenne, Bill, 1949-
    Joseph and the Coat of Many Colors/[story retold for this edition by Bill Yenne].
        p.   cm.—(Children's Bible Classics)
    ISBN 0-7852-8326-9 (MM)—ISBN 0-7852-8330-7 (TR)
    1. Joseph (Son of Jacob)—Juvenile literature.   2. Bible stories, English—O.T. Genesis.   [1. Joseph (Son of Jacob)
2. Bible Stories—O.T.]   I. Title.   II. Series.
BS580.J6Y46   1994
222'.1109505—dc20
                                                                                     93-37474
                                                                                     CIP
                                                                                     AC

94 95 96 97 98—1 2 3 4 5

Printed and bound in the United States of America

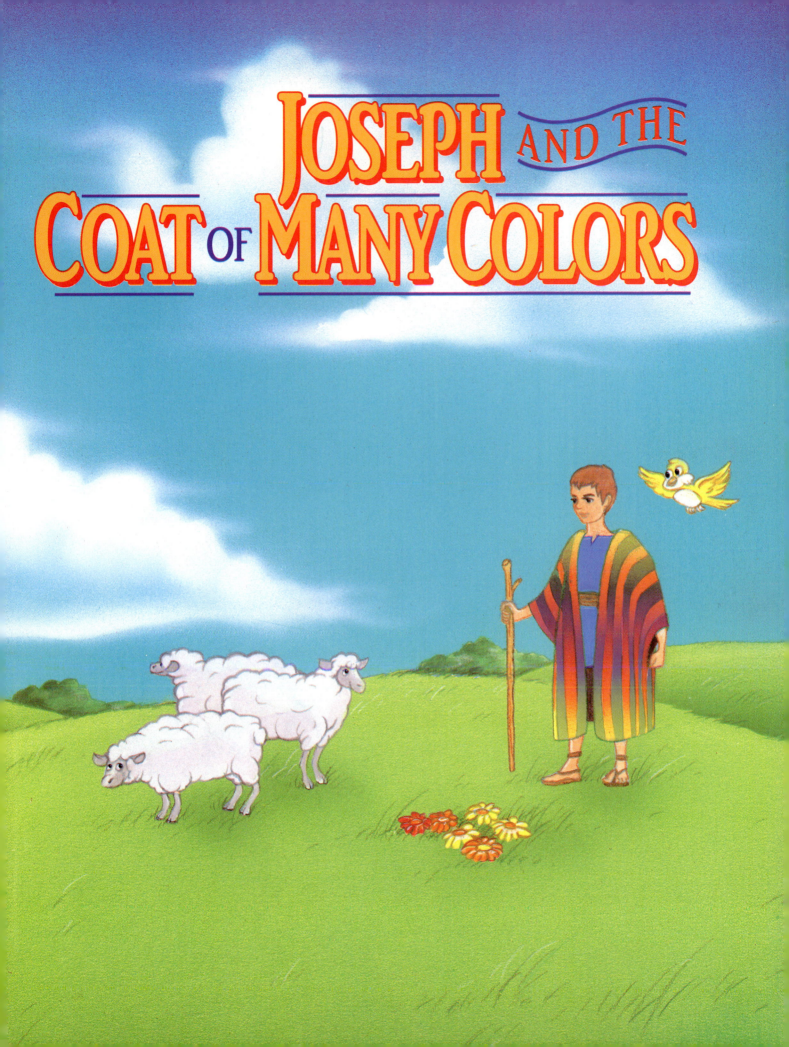

JOSEPH AND THE COAT OF MANY COLORS

A long time ago, in a land called Hebron, there lived a very good man named Jacob. He had twelve sons. Of all his sons, Jacob loved Joseph best. Jacob loved Joseph so much that he made him a beautiful coat that seemed to have every color of the rainbow in it. That coat became known as Joseph's "coat of many colors."

Joseph's brothers were jealous that their father loved Joseph more than the rest of them. They were angry at the special way Joseph was treated.

Then Joseph had two dreams that were so remarkable he had to tell his brothers about them. In one dream, his brothers' sheaves of grain were bowing down to Joseph's sheaf. His other dream was about the sun, moon and eleven stars bowing down to Joseph.

His brothers thought Joseph was lying and bragging about the dreams, and they hated him for it. But their father Jacob kept Joseph's dreams in mind.

A short time later, Joseph's brothers were tending sheep far from home. When they saw Joseph coming, his brothers made plans to kill him.

The oldest brother, Reuben, talked his brothers out of their plan to kill Joseph.

Instead, they took Joseph's coat and threw him into an empty well.

Reuben planned
to come back later
that night and
rescue Joseph from
the well. But before Reuben
could rescue Joseph, a group
of traders came by. Joseph's
other brothers decided that
they would sell Joseph into
slavery rather than kill him.
They sold him for 20 pieces
of silver.

When Reuben came back, he found out what his brothers had done. He was very upset.

The brothers tore Joseph's coat and dipped it in goat's blood. They showed their father Jacob the coat. Jacob was sure that a wild animal had eaten Joseph. He was terribly sad, and none of his family could comfort him.

The traders took Joseph to Egypt where they sold him to Potipher, the captain of Pharaoh's guard. Later, because Joseph was such a good man, Potipher made him the chief servant of his whole house.

Potipher's wife wanted Joseph to love her. But Joseph was loyal to Potipher and he would not obey Potipher's wife. She became very angry.

Potipher's wife made up a lie about Joseph, and Potipher had him thrown into jail. Even there, God took care of Joseph. The keeper of the jail put Joseph in charge of all the other prisoners.

Some years later, while Joseph was still in jail, Pharaoh had two strange dreams. None of his best advisers could figure out the dreams. Finally, a man who had been in prison remembered how Joseph had been able to tell what dreams meant. He told Pharaoh that Joseph could explain his dreams. Pharaoh sent for Joseph.

Joseph said the dream meant that Egypt would have seven years of good crops. Then seven years would pass when nothing would grow and there would be no food. Joseph said that Egypt should store up food from the good years to use when there were no crops.

Pharaoh was amazed at Joseph's wisdom. He made Joseph second in command over all of Egypt. Only Pharaoh himself would be more important than Joseph. Pharaoh gave Joseph fine clothes to wear. He put a gold chain around Joseph's neck and took his own ring and put it on Joseph's finger.

Joseph married an Egyptian girl and they had two sons.
The crops increased year by year, just as he had predicted.
There were seven good years for all the land.

Then the seven bad years came. The people were hungry and Pharaoh told all the people to go to Joseph and do whatever he said.

Joseph was now the governor of the land. He sold food to all who came. His father Jacob sent all of his brothers except Benjamin to buy food from Egypt. Joseph knew who they were, but Joseph's brothers didn't recognize him after twenty years.

Joseph decided to test his brothers to see if they had changed. Eventually, they proved that they had become much better men. But Joseph still did not tell them he was their brother.

After a while, the brothers came back for more food. This time they brought Benjamin. Joseph finally told them who he was. He told them that it was actually God's will that he was brought to live in Egypt.

Pharaoh heard the whole story and was very happy for Joseph. Pharaoh arranged with Joseph to have his family move to Egypt. They would share in the riches of Pharaoh's kingdom.

All of Joseph's relatives were happy to make the trip to Egypt. Best of all, Joseph's beloved father, Jacob, came with them. Jacob was very glad his son was still alive.

Joseph went out and met his father. They were very happy to see each other. Jacob lived for many more years. He gave his blessing to Joseph's sons. He knew they would be good men, just like their father, Joseph.